TELEVISION
THEN AND NOW

CYNTHIA KENNEDY HENZEL

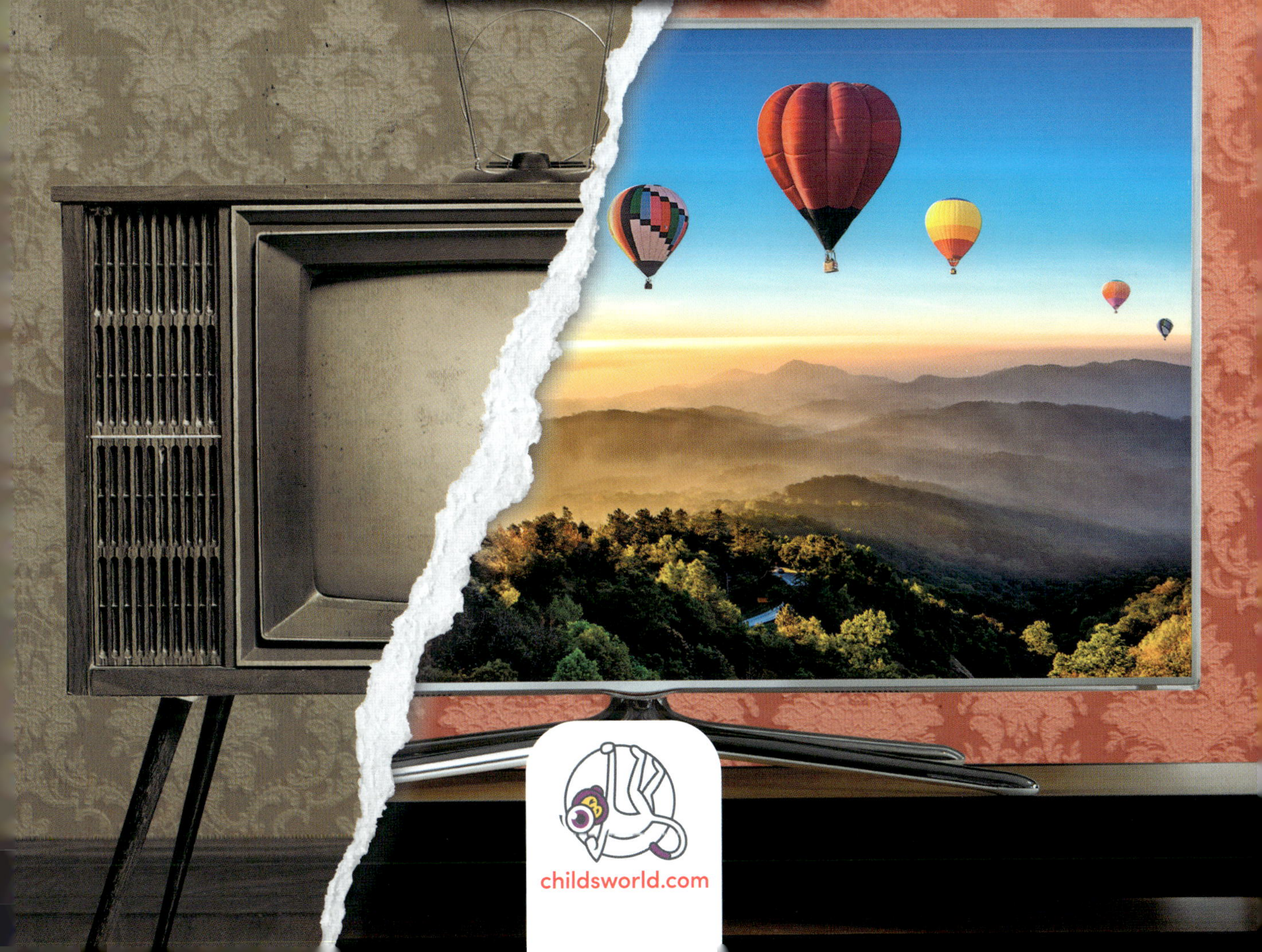

Published by The Child's World®
800-599-READ · www.childsworld.com

Photography Credits
Photographs ©: Shutterstock Images, cover (old TV), cover (modern TV), cover (background), cover (TV screen), cover (icon), 1 (old TV), 1 (modern TV), 1 (background), 1 (TV screen), 1 (icon), 3 (background), 3 (icon), 4, 17, 22; AP Images, 5; SSPL/Getty Images, 7; Archive Photos/Getty Images, 9; Joe Seer/Shutterstock Images, 10; Peter Gudella/Shutterstock Images, 13; Ljupco Smokovski/Shutterstock Images, 14–15; Andrey Popov/Shutterstock Images, 18; Red Line Editorial, 20

ISBN Information
9781503889538 (Reinforced Library Binding)
9781503891159 (Portable Document Format)
9781503892392 (Online Multi-user eBook)
9781503893634 (Electronic Publication)

LCCN 2023950240

Printed in the United States of America

Cynthia Kennedy Henzel has a BS in social studies education and an MS in geography. She has worked as a teacher-educator in many countries. Currently, she writes fiction and nonfiction books and develops educational materials for social studies, history, science, and ELL students. She has written more than 100 books and 150 stories for young people.

INTRODUCTION
THE HISTORY OF TELEVISION 4

CHAPTER 1
THE BIG THREE 6

CHAPTER 2
THE RISE OF CABLE 12

CHAPTER 3
STREAMING TV 16

Wonder More . . . 21

Fast Facts . . . 22

Glossary . . . 23

Find Out More . . . 24

Index . . . 24

TELEVISION

Several people contributed to the invention of television. These include Boris Rosing, Alan Archibald Campbell-Swinton, and John Logie Baird. In 1927, Philo Taylor Farnsworth invented the first television set. Television, or TV, has changed people's lives. Families watch TV together. TV introduces people to other cultures. People get their news from television. Companies sell their products on TV. Today, people have newer technology such as computers and smartphones. Still, the average American spends about 3 hours a day watching television.

Philo Taylor Farnsworth got the idea for the television when he was in high school.

THE BIG THREE

Early television **broadcasts** used an analog signal. This meant that a picture was scanned in thin rows. The picture and sound were then sent out as radio waves. An **antenna** received the signal. Then, the TV displayed the rows of the picture. Changing the rows rapidly made it look as though the picture was moving.

The Baird Televisor was an early TV set. It first sold in 1930.

Television's popularity did not begin to rise until after World War II (1939–1945). There were only three main TV **networks**. They were CBS, NBC, and ABC. People did not have to pay to get TV signals. The networks made money by selling **advertising**. Companies made advertisements, or commercials, about their products to show during programs. They often used short, catchy songs called jingles.

Popular programs included funny shows about families. These were called situation comedies, or sitcoms. An early successful sitcom was *I Love Lucy*. It was about a housewife, Lucy Ricardo, and her bandleader husband Ricky.

Actress Lucille Ball starred in *I Love Lucy*. She also performed in radio shows and movies.

Other popular shows were about detectives, doctors, or cowboys. During the day, the networks showed **soap operas** and game shows. People liked to watch their favorite characters. The number of homes with televisions grew from 6,000 in 1946 to 45.7 million in 1960.

Actor LeVar Burton starred in *Roots* and later hosted a children's program on PBS.

HOWDY DOODY

The first TV program for children, *Howdy Doody*, began in 1947. Howdy Doody was a puppet. The program was hosted by a man named Buffalo Bob Smith and featured many characters.

PBS became the fourth big network in the late 1960s. PBS did not have commercials. It was funded by the government, companies, and viewers. PBS showed **educational** programs. Many were about history or nature. It also presented children's programs, such as *Sesame Street*.

By the 1970s, programs became more **diverse**. *The Mary Tyler Moore Show* was about working women. The series *Roots* was about Black history in the United States.

Network programs were broadcast on a **schedule**. Everyone watched the same shows at the same time every day. People often spent family time watching TV. The next day, people talked about yesterday's programs with friends.

THE RISE OF CABLE

TVs with antennas did not always work well. Analog signals got weaker the farther they traveled. Weak signals introduced **interference** to TV images. Sometimes the picture looked fuzzy. People had to turn their antennas in different directions to get a better picture.

Some communities with poor signals put a large antenna in a high place. This picked up a signal from a nearby city. Then, people paid to connect to the antenna through underground cables.

Cable communities could receive more than programs from national networks.

One common kind of TV interference is sometimes called static, noise, or snow.

They received local broadcasts, such as local sports. Soon, large companies realized that people would pay to have more programs. The first paid cable service, HBO, began showing movies in 1975. The sports network ESPN and the children's network Nickelodeon both began in 1979. The first cable news network, CNN, began 24-hour news programs the next year. MTV, which showed music videos, began in 1981.

Videotape recorders became popular in the 1980s. People could record shows on tape to watch later. They could go to the store and rent videotapes to play on their TVs. People could choose what to watch and when to watch it.

People wished that their analog TV screens could be bigger. The largest screen for an analog signal was 42 inches (107 cm) wide. Plus, picture tubes were heavy. Televisions came in large wooden cabinets. They sat on the floor. Some TV cabinets were as big as a couch.

In the 1990s, a new technology called digital TV (DTV) appeared. Digital signals sent information the way a computer does. The picture was displayed in pixels instead of rows. Pixels are tiny squares that change color. When seen together, they make a picture.

Flat-screen TVs can be mounted on walls to save space in a room.

Digital signals could carry much more information than analog signals. This soon led to high-definition TV (HDTV). HDTV had a sharper picture and better sound than analog TV. New screen technology, such as liquid-crystal display (LCD), could show these pictures. LCD TVs had large screens, but they were flat and lightweight.

STREAMING TV

By the 2020s, lots of people watched TV by streaming. Streaming is sending video and sound signals over the internet. The internet is a network of computers that share information. Smart TVs connect directly to the internet. Streaming services, such as Netflix, began in the mid-2000s. Lots of TV shows are released only on streaming services. Other shows are broadcast on TV as well as streamed.

Many streaming services offer programs for children and families.

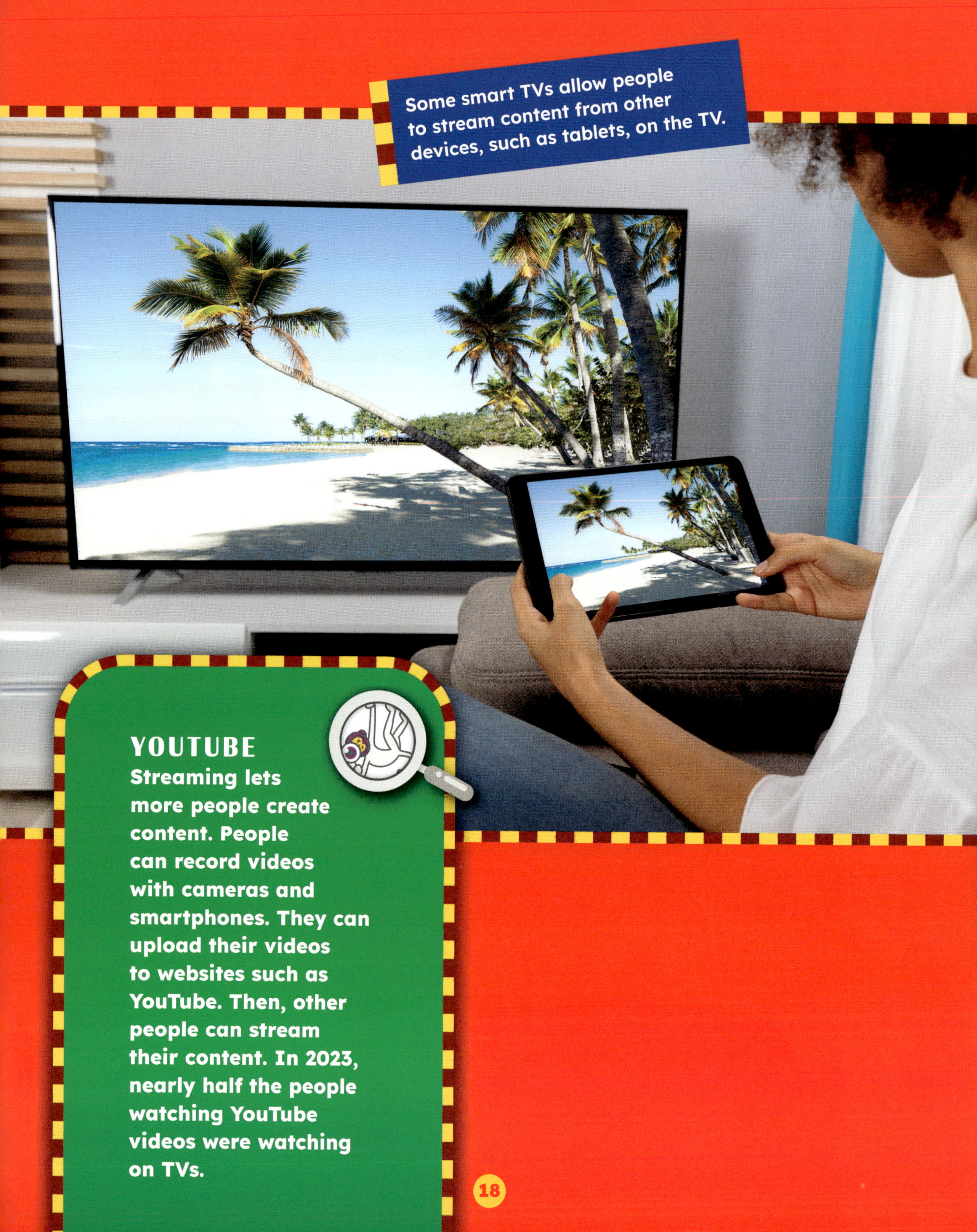

Some smart TVs allow people to stream content from other devices, such as tablets, on the TV.

YOUTUBE

Streaming lets more people create content. People can record videos with cameras and smartphones. They can upload their videos to websites such as YouTube. Then, other people can stream their content. In 2023, nearly half the people watching YouTube videos were watching on TVs.

Streaming services don't have a schedule. They are on demand. This means people can watch any available show or movie at any time. Streaming services are usually less expensive than cable. However, streaming services might not have all the shows people want. Streaming also requires a good internet connection.

People can stream content to their computers, phones, and other devices. But many people still stream to their TVs. Newer TVs have amazingly sharp pictures. Ultra-high-definition (UHD) TVs have four times the number of pixels of HDTVs. Other TVs use organic light-emitting diodes (OLED) instead of LCD. These TVs show more colors and **contrast**. They can be even thinner and lighter than LCD TVs.

How People Watch TV

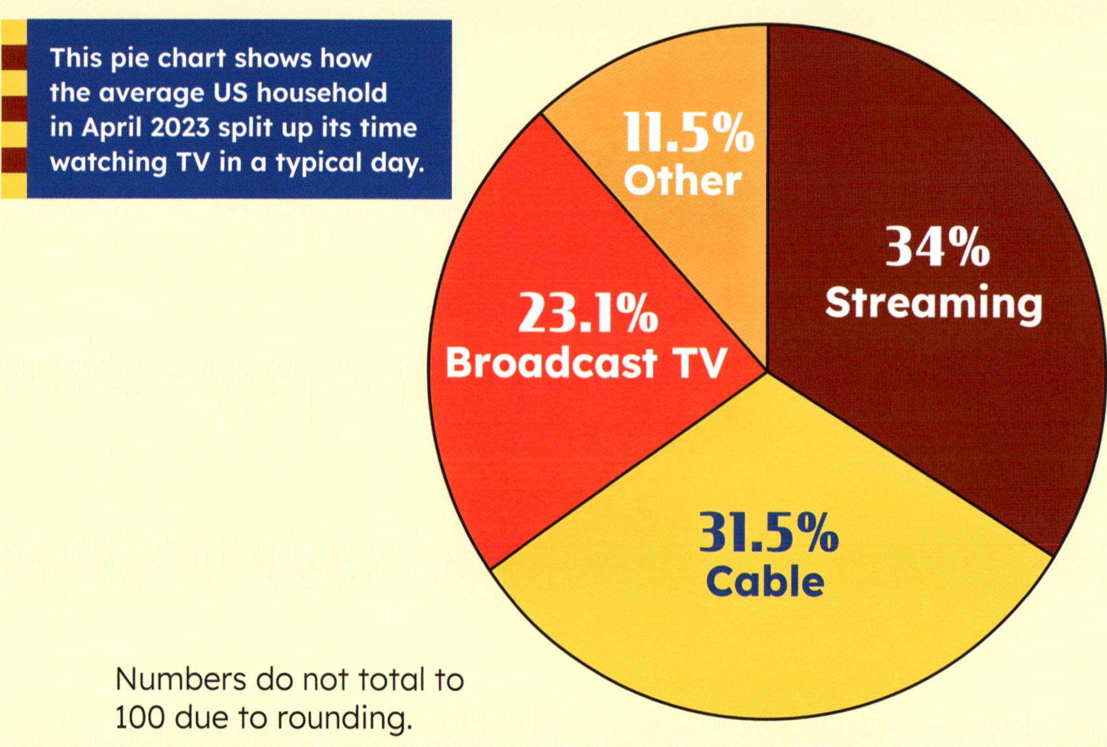

Numbers do not total to 100 due to rounding.

In the future, television may include virtual reality (VR) technology. VR technology uses screens inside headsets. It makes people feel as though they are inside other worlds. People may be able to interact with their favorite shows. There is a lot of change to look forward to in the future of television.

WONDER MORE

Wondering about New Information

How much did you know about the history of television before reading this book? What new information did you learn? Write down three new facts that this book taught you. Was the new information surprising? Why or why not?

Wondering How It Matters

What is one positive way that television affects your life? What is one negative way that television affects your life? If you cannot think of a positive or negative effect, imagine how television might affect other kids. What impact might television have on their lives?

Wondering Why

TV shows have become more diverse since the first shows were broadcast. Why do you think it is important for TV shows to be diverse? How do you think people feel when they see characters who look like them on TV?

Ways to Keep Wondering

After reading this book, what questions do you have about television today? What can you do to learn more about television?

FAST FACTS

- Several people, including Boris Rosing, Alan Archibald Campbell-Swinton, and John Logie Baird, invented early television technology.
- Philo Taylor Farnsworth invented the first television set in 1927.
- Most people in the United States did not have TVs until the 1950s and 1960s.
- Early analog TVs used an antenna to receive pictures and sound sent as radio waves.
- Analog signals often suffered from interference.
- Cable TV sends signals through underground wires.
- Cable networks gave most viewers access to more programs than they had before.
- Digital TV sends information the way a computer does.
- LCD or OLED screens can display digital TV pictures.
- Digital TV allows the use of thinner, smaller, lighter screens that show sharper pictures.
- Streaming is sending pictures and sound to TVs through the internet.
- People can stream shows and movies on demand.

GLOSSARY

advertising (AD-ver-ty-zing) Advertising is the content used to sell a product or service. TV commercials are a form of advertising.

antenna (an-TEN-uh) An antenna is a device used to receive radio or television signals. Early TVs received signals using an antenna.

broadcasts (BRAWD-kastz) Broadcasts are radio or television transmissions. TV news broadcasts provide lots of people with information about current events.

contrast (KON-trast) Contrast is the difference between the brightest and darkest colors that a screen can produce. People adjust the contrast on their screens to get the best-looking picture.

diverse (dy-VERSE) Something is diverse if it includes people from different social or ethnic backgrounds. TV audiences seek diverse programs.

educational (ed-yoo-KAY-shuh-nuhl) Educational means helping people learn. Many kids learn from educational TV programs.

interference (in-tur-FEER-ens) Interference is the disruption of TV signals. Early TVs often suffered from interference.

networks (NET-werks) Television networks are large companies that provide content for TV. NBC and CBS are TV networks.

schedule (SKED-jool) A schedule is a list of events and the times when they are supposed to happen. TV networks broadcast shows on a schedule.

soap operas (SOHP AH-pur-uhz) Soap operas are dramatic shows about the daily lives of a group of characters. Soap operas have been on TV since the 1940s.

FIND OUT MORE

In the Library

Bethea, Nikole Brooks. *TVs and Remote Controls*. Minneapolis, MN: Jump!, 2021.

Green, Sara. *The Television*. Minneapolis, MN: Bellwether Media, 2022.

Swanson, Jennifer. *How Does the Internet Work?* Parker, CO: The Child's World, 2022.

On the Web

Visit our website for links about television:
childsworld.com/links

Note to Parents, Caregivers, Teachers, and Librarians: We routinely verify our web links to make sure they are safe and active sites. So encourage your readers to check them out!

INDEX

cable TV, 12–13, 19

digital TV, 14–15

Farnsworth, Philo Taylor, 4

Howdy Doody, 10

I Love Lucy, 8

LCD TVs, 15, 19

Netflix, 16

PBS, 11
pixels, 14, 19

Roots, 11

Sesame Street, 11
smartphones, 4, 18–19
streaming, 16–19

virtual reality (VR), 20

YouTube, 18